A Note from the Author

Bonsai that straddle the small-to-miniature category reach about 8 inches (20cm) in height and can take up to 20 years to fully mature. The term "miniature bonsai" generally refers to bonsai small enough to be lifted or moved with one hand. The term "super-mini bonsai" refers to the smallest plants in the miniature bonsai category; of these, the smallest plants can fit on a fingertip and grow in a pot no larger than a thimble. While cultivating bonsai is a slow process, super-mini bonsai can be enjoyed as soon they're potted—and these plants are simple and satisfying to grow and to pot. They take up virtually no space at all, so they can add a little touch of green in unexpected places. What's more, if properly cared for they can last for years, continuing to give pleasure as they change and grow. While "bonsai" carries with it the impression of being a hobby for someone with plenty of free time, mini bonsai gardening is a actually a great hobby for busy people, novices at gardening, and anyone who enjoys working with small plants. Though the plants are tiny, growing them is a complete gardening experience. Why not give super-mini bonsai a try?

MINIATURE
BONSAI

The Complete Guide to Super-Mini Bonsai

Terutoshi Iwai

TUTTLE Publishing

Tokyo | Rutland, Vermont | Singapore

CONTENTS

Chapter 1

The Basics of Super-mini Bonsai and How to Prepare Them

Chapter 2

Making Super-mini Bonsai

Chapter 3

Super-mini Bonsai Maintenance

Chapter 4

Displaying and Enjoying Super-mini Bonsai

Chapter 5

All Kinds of Super-mini Bonsai

Tiny Little Bonsai
That Fit on a Fingertip

Super-mini bonsai are only about an inch or so (3cm) tall but have huge appeal. Even though they're tiny, they put out roots and grow just as a regular plant does.

Dragon's blood cactus (succulent family)

Experience the Real Pleasure that a Genuine Bonsai Brings

One of the enjoyable things about bonsai is being able to shape it to your tastes while you care for the branches and foliage. Super-mini bonsai allow you to fully experience the pleasures associated with bonsai.

Cotoneaster

Sprout an Acorn and Enjoy Watching it Grow

When making super-mini bonsai, use shoots grown from acorns and other seeds or cuttings with root growth as nursery stock. Seeing the daily changes such as the growth of buds or roots is sure to become a daily source of pleasure.

Chinese cork oak (Quercus variabilis) at one year (left) and at three years (right).

A silk tree (Albizia julibrissin) and acorn planted together.

Flowering crab apple (Malus halliana)

Chinese elm (Ulmus parvifolia)

Enjoy the Four Seasons, Super-mini Style

Buds forming, flowers blooming, leaves changing color and then falling... the seasons change like this even in the world inside a little plant pot. Super-mini bonsai are nature in miniature, letting you experience the four seasons at close range.

Have Fun Decorating Your Home with Super-mini Bonsai

Place them on little plates or coasters, line them up next to miniature figures—there are no rules when it comes to super-mini bonsai. They lend themselves to whatever decorating ideas come to mind. Thinking of ways to display them is part of the fun.

Chinese fringe tree (Chionanthus retusus)

Flowering crab apple (Malus halliana)

Designing Super-mini Bonsai to Your Own Taste

Once you get the hang of things, you'll be able to shape super-mini bonsai or display them however you like. Super-mini bonsai are little works of art, so enjoy choosing the materials to use and the pleasure of creating expression through form.

Japanese white pine (Pinus parviflora)

Chapter 1

The Basics of Super-mini Bonsai and How to Prepare Them

In this chapter we've listed in detail the requirements and preparation needed for creating super-mini bonsai, which will allow you to get a better idea of what can be achieved. Make sure to check these pages when you start creating your own super-mini bonsai.

Chinese cork oak
(Quercus variabilis)

Japanese maple
(Acer palmatum aka shidare)

Chinese quince
(Pseudocydonia sinensis)

What are Super-mini Bonsai?

Many people may know the word "bonsai" but aren't really sure what it means. Before you start, it's helpful to become familiar with the basics of bonsai.

Easy to manage, small and charming

Bonsai can be divided into several categories depending on their size. Broadly speaking, they are usually divided as shown on the right, into large, medium and small sizes. Of these, the small bonsai are easier to manage than the large ones, and "bonsai that fit in the palm of the hand" have become popular recently.

Among the small bonsai, the particularly tiny ones are called mini bonsai, *mame* [bean-size] bonsai and so on. Super-mini bonsai are even smaller than these. In this book, super-mini bonsai are about an inch (3cm), give or take, in height and width, but rather than adhering to a strict measurement, we'll define these as bonsai that are small enough to fit onto the tip of a finger or be held in between the fingertips.

TYPES OF BONSAI

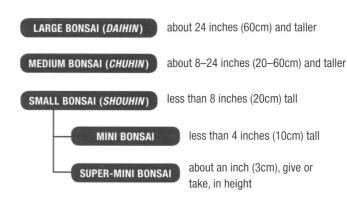

LARGE BONSAI (*DAIHIN*) about 24 inches (60cm) and taller

MEDIUM BONSAI (*CHUHIN*) about 8–24 inches (20–60cm) and taller

SMALL BONSAI (*SHOUHIN*) less than 8 inches (20cm) tall

MINI BONSAI less than 4 inches (10cm) tall

SUPER-MINI BONSAI about an inch (3cm), give or take, in height

Regular small bonsai Mini bonsai Super-mini bonsai

TIDBIT

The History of Bonsai

Bonsai are said to have been brought to Japan from missions in the Sui and Tang dynasties (between the 6th and 10th centuries CE). During the Heian period (794–1185 CE), the aristocracy cultivated an appreciation of potted plants, and in the Kamakura period (1185–1333) various tree species and types of pots came into use. In the Edo period (1603–1868), this appreciation spread from the *daimyo* (feudal lords) to the common townsfolk and it is thought that the term "bonsai" began to be used during this time.

Building on this, further developments in the Meiji pe-

riod (1868–1912) led to the establishment of an intrinsically Japanese view of art that defines bonsai as we know it today: that is, "the expression of nature's grandeur and beauty in a small vessel, and the appreciation of this."

In recent years, particularly in the US, bonsai fans have rapidly increased in number. Even in Japan, where until recently bonsai was commonly seen as a hobby for older people, it has become popular people of all ages. As they are easier to access than traditional bonsai, the creation of super-mini bonsai can be considered a natural development within the overall trend.

Japanese winterberry (Ilex serrata)

Cherry (Prunus)

Snowrose (Serissa japonica)

Princess pussy willow

Weeping forsythia
(Forsythia suspensa)

Japanese white pine (Pinus parviflora)

Spindle tree (Euonymus fortunei)

What's So Appealing about Super-mini Bonsai?

Why do I recommend super-mini bonsai? How do they differ from larger bonsai, or from flowers, ornamental plants and other regular potted plants? Let's dig further into their appeal.

Tiny little bonsai just an inch or so (3cm) tall

A bonsai is essentially a potted plant whose trunk and branches are artfully adjusted for the purpose of fostering a deep appreciation of nature. It differs from a regular potted plant in that its form is trained so as to represent a natural landscape within a confined space.

It takes years of work to achieve the desired shape and effect. Growing a bonsai to maturity requires not only time, but also space and financial investment, and so bonsai gardening has tended to be the province of people for whom such factors are not much of an issue.

Super-mini bonsai came about because they are easier to create, require less time and can be worked on even in small spaces. Once the plant has been propagated, a super-mini bonsai can be potted, displayed and admired immediately. Like other plants, super-mini bonsai require regular care and, if properly maintained, will give years of enjoyment. Super-mini bonsai combine the magic of growing

things with the magic of small things. They are fun to display and, whether placed singly or arranged in multiples, are sure to captivate.

A creeping plant is wound round and round in this "winding super-mini bonsai." It's a project just right for beginners (see page 34).

The fun of creating them

Part of bonsai's special appeal is the process of guiding the trunk and other parts of the plant into whatever shape you like. It's easy to get started on super-mini bonsai.

The fun of growing them

Left uncared for, super-mini bonsai immediately start to weaken, Properly looked after, they will grow for years, and their various changes over time will be a source of pleasure.

At the left is a one-year-old pine tree, while the trees on the right have two years of growth. While they're small, over time their characteristics start to show.

Trim branches with the desired form in mind. Once you get used to it, this becomes an enjoyable pastime (see page 48).

The fun of displaying them

Super-mini bonsai have a sweet appeal. They can be easily displayed to great effect in containers you have in hand such as small transparent cases and little dishes.

The more plants you line up, the more fun and varied the effect. Display them on window ledges, on top of shelves, in the kitchen and anywhere else you like.

Making Super-mini Bonsai

Although super-mini bonsai are much easier to create than larger bonsai, they cannot be completed in just a day or two. But the process is a big part of the appeal. Dedicate some time to making super-mini bonsai, appreciate their transformation and have fun as you go.

Start by growing a seedling

The kinds of little potted plants used for super-mini bonsai are not sold in stores, so you will need to prepare them yourself. Broadly speaking, there are two ways to do this. The first is by taking cuttings and planting them in soil to encourage root growth. The other way is to grow plants from seed.

Some plants that are used for super-mini bonsai, such as ivy and other creepers and vines, can be used immediately after gathering, but for the most part, it takes anywhere from a month to a year until a plant grown from a cutting or from seed is ready for use.

Potted plants don't have to be made into super-mini bonsai straight away—it's fine to grow some simply as potted plants. But if you have a few potted plants ready-grown, you can make as many super-mini bonsai as you like, whenever you like.

Creating, growing and displaying your super-mini bonsai

Once the seedlings have been propagated, it's time to create super-mini bonsai, starting with transferring the plants into small pots. Regular bonsai require years to reach the stage where they can be displayed, but once super-mini bonsai have been transferred into their pots, they are complete. What's more, they offer all the charms unique to bonsai, such as allowing their branches to be shaped and bearing flowers and fruit.

Watered daily, fertilized and disinfected regularly, and with proper maintenance of branches and roots, bonsai can be enjoyed for years. They are not common houseplants, though. They should be grown outdoors and, once potted, should spend as much time outdoors as weather and other conditions will allow.

TIDBIT

Don't Little Bonsai Grow Bigger?

Super-mini bonsai planted in little pots do not grow big as they would if planted outdoors. Even garden trees that can grow as tall as a person remain small when grown in a little pot.

However, to keep raising them for a long period of time, it's necessary to repot super-mini bonsai regularly. Removing them from the pot, maintaining the roots and replacing the soil allows even these small plants to properly put out roots and absorb nutrients that ensure robust growth.

Grown in a little pot, this super-mini Japanese maple tree bonsai stays small.

Growing the Plant Prior to Creating the Super-mini Bonsai

SEARCHING FOR POTENTIAL POTTED PLANTS

Potential super-mini bonsai can be grown from cuttings or from seed. Cuttings can be taken from garden trees, potted plants and so on, while seeds can be found in gardens, parks and wooded areas along with acorns, pine cones and the like (see page 18).

PROPAGATING SEEDLINGS

Depending on the type of tree or plant used, a seedling can put out strong roots within as little time as one month to be ready for use as a super-mini bonsai. Grow a few potted plants at a time so that you can turn them into super-mini bonsai whenever you like (see pages 20–24).

CREATING SUPER-MINI BONSAI

Once the potted plant is ready, making a super-mini bonsai takes no time at all. A simple super-mini bonsai is complete as soon as it's been transferred into a little pot! For authentic trained trunks and branches or to create interesting shapes, use wire and position as desired (see chapter 2).

GROWING SUPER-MINI BONSAI

Super-mini bonsai should be grown outdoors. With some effort, a suitable growing environment can be created on a balcony or even smaller space, or of course in the garden. Fertilizing and disinfecting the plants, killing insects and pests, caring for the branches and looking after the roots and soil by transferring the plants regularly will encourage healthy growth (see chapter 3).

Acorns being grown into seedlings.

A Japanese box tree cutting taken from the garden.

Seedlings grown from acorns. These have been grown with the acorns above ground.

The Japanese box tree seedling is transferred to a pot to create a super-mini bonsai.

DISPLAYING SUPER-MINI BONSAI

Display your super-mini bonsai indoors when you want to add some greenery to your everyday life. Although they're small, they have a presence that calms and soothes (see chapter 4).

Watering super-mini bonsai. They require little space for maintenance.

It's fun thinking of ways to display your work.

Materials and Tools

Necessary materials and tools can be assembled from items on hand,
hardware stores, gardening centers and online vendors.

Finding materials and tools suited to small pots and delicate operations

Fine-grained soil suitable for small pots and tools such as tweezers that make delicate tasks easier are used for super-mini bonsai creation and maintenance. There's no need to have all manner of items on hand, just prepare the basics to start with, and then if you later decide to continue with super-mini bonsai, you can purchase more specialist equipment.

The items here are the must-haves for creating super-mini bonsai: soil, tools and pots. Have sphagnum moss on hand as well, and if you want to stabilize branches or shape the bonsai, wire will be necessary also. Make a list of what you need and assemble those items so that they'll be at your fingertips.

| SOILS | Use a soil mix. For super-mini bonsai, whichever type of soil you choose, use the smallest grain possible such as "extra fine" or "fine-grain." |

Breathability and moisture retention are critical

The balance of breathability, moisture retention and drainage need to be considered when it comes to soil, resulting in a mix such as this one. Keep the mixed soil in a conveniently sized, sealable container. The lid of the container is perfect as a work surface when making the super-mini bonsai, and a plastic dessert spoon kept in the container, makes a convenient scoop.

❶ Hard akadama (extra-fine grain)—60%
Akadama soil is soil in granule form, made from sifting the Kanto region's loam layer. The hard quality type does not crush easily and has excellent breathability, moisture retention and drainage properties.
❷ Fuji sand—20%
This is volcanic soil from Mt Fuji. It has excellent moisture retention properties.
❸ Yahagi river sand (size 1)—20%
This river sand is from the Chubu region. The grains do not crush easily and it drains well.

TOOLS	The basic tools for bonsai are all available at hardware and DIY stores. Once you get the hang of things, you can start to purchase other tools.

Scissors, tweezers and pliers make up the basic 3-piece tool set

When you're just starting out, all you need are scissors, tweezers and pliers. Scissors and tweezers in particular can also be used in caring for potted plants.

❶ Pliers: tools to cut the wire that is used to stabilize branches.
❷ Scissors: used for pruning branches.
❸ Tweezers: used to grip foliage or pack soil in firmly.

Helpful extras

❶ Radio pliers: used to bend wire into shape.
❷ Branch cutter: used to cut branches neatly at their base.
❸ Root cutter: scissors used specifically for trimming roots.

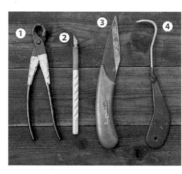

Getting serious

❶ Knob cutter: used for trimming knobs from trees.
❷ Cutter knife: used for shaving and smoothing off the trunk after cutting off branches.
❸ Scalpel: used for shaving off layers on a trunk and so on.
❹ Root hook: used for loosening roots.

SPHAGNUM MOSS AND OTHER MOSSES	Mosses are used when planting super-mini bonsai. They are all around, but make sure you never run out of them at a crucial moment by always having some on hand.

Sphagnum moss

Used for covering the soil in a pot, sphagnum moss acts as a lid to prevent soil spilling from the pot or drying out. It can be purchased at DIY, hardware and all-purpose stores.

Moss

Moss is planted over the sphagnum moss that covers the soil. Apart from being attractive, it acts as a guide for watering.

POTS

Small pots are really adorable, and looking for them is part of the fun of bonsai. They come in various shapes, colors and patterns.

Finding the right pot for you

In the art of bonsai, the pot forms part of the completed work. The goal is to have a pot that is in harmony with the tree. Various kinds of pots made from different mediums and in different shapes may be used to complement the tree varieties and forms.

Just as for large bonsai, pots are available for little bonsai and are known as *mame* (bean) pots due to their small size, but they may not be readily available near you. When making super-mini bonsai, don't limit yourself to using bonsai pots. Instead, use small containers that freely express your own sense of style.

UNIQUE ARTISAN PIECES

Mame pots made by ceramic artists can be found on their home pages and so on. As they are one-off works, they may be slightly expensive, but even though they are small, they are good quality, attractive pieces.

MACHINE MADE POTS

These simply formed pots are inexpensive and easily accessible. Apart from being stocked at bonsai stores, they are also sold at bonsai fairs and events.

UNUSUAL POTS

When viewing and researching small bonsai, you may come across unusual pots such as those shaped like roof tiles, books and so on. Part of the experience is using a pot you really like.

THESE CAN BE POTS TOO!

Here, I've used a beautiful shell instead of a pot. As there is no hole in the base, watering can be tricky, but if the plant is sturdy then it should grow without any trouble.

Creating a Pot Using Items on Hand

Pots for super-mini bonsai are not limited to what is sold in stores.
Use items you have on hand to make original pots that are always at the ready.

Pots that make bonsai care easier

Pots with a hole in the base are best as they make watering and drainage easier. However, for sturdy plants such as ivy and succulents which do not need as much attention when it comes to water, it's possible to use pots that don't have holes.

Bear in mind that although they are small, super-mini bonsai can grow to two or more times the height of a tiny pot. Adjust your pot if necessary to ensure a stable base and avoid tipover.

POT IDEA 1

Make a hole in a little vessel

Try making a hole in a little dish or plate to use as a pot. It's possible to make a hole in earthenware or pottery, but porcelain is not suitable for this as it will break.

① Wet and wring it out a rag and place it on the ground or a stable surface, then place the vessel upside down on top of the rag.
② Place the sharp end of a nail on the spot where the hole is needed and tap lightly with a hammer. The trick is to not use too much force but to tap the same spot over and over again.

After about 100 patient taps, a neat hole is formed.

POT IDEA 2

Add feet to a thimble

Thimbles have rounded bases and are easily tipped over, so use pottery cement to add feet at four spots for stability. It's fine to make a drainage hole too, but some thimbles may crack easily so it's OK to leave them intact.

A thimble with feet made from pottery cement.

Souvenir thimbles from overseas have pretty patterns and are perfect as pots.

Preparing the Seedling

Here, "seedling" refers to a plant used to make a super-mini bonsai.
They are small and not sold in shops, so must be grown from cuttings or from seed.

Acquiring and growing seedlings

The method of acquiring and propagating plant stocks depends on whether they are taken from cuttings or grown from seed.

First of all, to propagate cuttings, trim off branches or stalks from garden plants and pot plants to use as stock. Creepers such as ivy are available as ornamental plants and are easy to acquire as well as being robust and easy to grow, so are recommended for beginners.

When growing plants from seed, acorns, pine cones and the like can be found in parks and wooded areas and grown into seedlings. Be careful never to take things from people's gardens without permission and do not remove items from conservation areas and places where such behavior is banned.

In Japan, removing plants is not permitted in any mountain area. Keep the preservation of nature in mind and gather plants in the spirit of gratefully accepting a small amount of nature's bounty.

Once you have grown the cuttings and seeds you have acquired to the point where they are putting out roots and shoots, they can be used as plant stock for super-mini bonsai.

After a year, this Japanese box tree cutting has grown considerably.

TIDBIT

How should moss be prepared?

Moss is used to spread over the soil when making super-mini bonsai.

Sphagnum moss is generally sold in a dehydrated state. You can buy living moss, but purchasable varieties may be limited, and your chances of having the right moss for your bonsai are better if you propagate your own. Take some that was used for other bonsai or gather it from parks or woodlands, then place it in a shallow container on top of damp newspaper in a shaded spot. Propagate your moss when you propagate your seedlings to be sure you have some ready to be harvested when needed.

The moss shown here is Brachymenium exile which grows all over Japan. It's best to use moss that doesn't grow too high.

Take cuttings from garden and potted trees

Plants that lend themselves to being grown from cuttings include those that do not produce seeds and those which take a long time to grow into usable seedlings. These include Japanese box, spindle trees, weeping forsythia, Deutzia and other small trees (see page 69) along with cedars, Chinese junipers and other coniferous trees associated with bonsai (see page 68).

The best time to take cuttings is around March before trees come into bud and around June when branches become tougher. The new buds at the ends of branches are soft and decay easily, so cut a length of 2–3 nodes from an old branch. Strip the lower leaves from this length to use as a cutting. It depends on the type of tree, but the cutting will put out roots in about a month to a year and develop into a cutting seedling (see page 20).

Weeping forsythia grown from a cutting.

Juniper grown from a cutting.

Start seedlings from acorns and pine cones

Plants suited to being propagated from seed include fruiting plants and those which have easily gathered seeds. For example, the acorns from pin oaks, sawtooth oaks and Chinese cork oaks are the plants' seeds. Acorns can be gathered in parks and woodlands around November–December, but it's fun having a go at propagating seeds of fruit closer to hand such as mango pits once the fruit has been eaten. The seeds of Japanese maples, trident maples and so on can be gathered in the fall and kept in a cool place with their wing sections stripped away.

Plants propagated from seed grow at different rates, with some sprouting as soon as the seed is sown, others taking a year to grow from a seed to a seedling and others not sprouting until the year after they are planted, or even longer. Once the seed has been sown and the plant has put out roots and buds, it becomes a seedling (see page 22).

Hornbeam seedlings.

Japanese maple seedlings.

GROWING SEEDLINGS FROM CUTTINGS

Branches and other sections cut from trees are planted in soil to take root and put forth new buds. Here, I've used the Japanese box.

You will need
- Cuttings
- Pot (about 6" wide)
- Soil (potting mix)
- Plant activator

Tools
- Scissors
- Tweezers
- Saucer (big enough to hold cuttings)
- Bucket or large container (to hold plenty of water)

Plants from cuttings

Preparing the cuttings

New buds (the light color at the tip of a stem) are soft and decay easily, so when taking cuttings, cut from below the previous year's growth.

Strip off leaves from the lower part of the branch.

Dilute some plant activator with water in the saucer (here we have used Medenel to 100 parts water) and place the cuttings in it for a few hours.

Preparing the soil

Fill pot with soil.

Fill bucket with water and place pot so water reaches 9/10 of the way up, allowing water to be absorbed through the hole in the base.

The soil after absorbing water.

● Planting the cuttings

Use tweezers to make holes in the soil at regular intervals.

Plant cuttings in holes.

TIP

Plant cuttings so they are neither too far apart nor crowded together, but rather have just enough space between them that they do not touch one another. If they are too far apart, they will be blown around by the wind and become unstable.

Use tweezers to fill in soil around the roots of the cuttings to stabilize them.

● Soaking the pot

Fill a bucket with water and soak the pot in it to absorb water.

● Place in the shade

For a week after planting, place in shadow out of sunlight and monitor progress.

● Done

The Japanese box puts out roots after a year, at which time it can be used as seedlings.

TIDBIT

How do I check whether the plant has put out roots?

The only way to know whether a plant has properly put out roots is to remove it from the ground. However, plants bud at the same time as they put out roots, so once new buds appear, it's safe to assume it has started to take root. It's useful to know roughly to what extent various species of plants put out roots.

GROWING PLANTS FROM SEEDS (GERMINATION)

Growing plants from seed is known as germination. Here, I've used sawtooth and pin oaks.

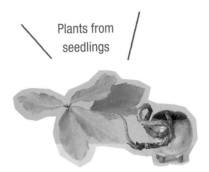
Plants from seedlings

Prepare seed bed

Fill pot with soil.

Fill bucket with water and place pot so water reaches 9/10 of the way up, allowing water to be absorbed through the hole in the base.

The soil after absorbing water.

Plant acorns

Lightly press acorns into soil at regular intervals.

The acorns after planting (the long ones are pin oaks, the round ones are sawtooth oaks).

TIP

It's OK to mix varieties when planting acorns, it's fine to mix various types in the one pot. Just plant whichever you have been able to find or the kind that you like.

● Cover with soil

TIP

Spread soil lightly over small seeds such as those of Japanese maples, make sure they won't be washed away when watering by covering them with a layer of soil about 2–3 times the depth of the seeds themselves.

Cover with soil about the thickness of an acorn.

Lightly press with your hand to stabilize.

● Done

Complete by watering. Place outside until roots start to develop and make sure to water sufficiently.

TIDBIT

Yearly transplanting is necessary

Whether you propagate plants from cuttings or seedlings, if you leave them as potted plants rather than using them for super-mini bonsai it is necessary to transplant them after a year. One of the reasons for this is that once the roots have spread throughout the pot, they won't be able to grow longer and the plant's growth will be negatively affected. Another reason is that the soil clumps, making it more difficult for water and air to permeate the soil. Repotting plants enables them to be propagated for a long time.

GERMINATING SEEDS IN SPHAGNUM MOSS

Germinating seeds in moist sphagnum moss results in winding roots which can be incorporated into the composition of the super-mini bonsai.

You will need
- Acorns
- Sphagnum moss
- Plastic bag

Tools
- Scissors

TIDBIT

When is it best to germinate seeds in sphagnum moss?

It's fine to germinate seeds as soon as you find them, but if you keep them indoors, they will start sprouting in winter, so it's best to keep them as seeds until the start of spring and germinate them in March.

● Prepare sphagnum moss —

Use scissors to finely shred sphagnum moss. Place in water and lightly wring out.

● Add acorns and close bag

Place sphagnum moss in plastic bag and add acorns.

Wring opening of plastic bag and secure firmly.

● Once the seeds put out roots

After about three weeks, roots start to appear.

Seeds germinated in sphagnum moss. From left: sawtooth oak, camellia, pin oak.

● Repotting

Once roots have appeared, plants can be made into super-mini bonsai, but if they are repotted their shape and form will develop still further.

Chapter 2

Making Super-mini Bonsai

Once you've got the tools and plant stock ready,
it's finally time to make super-mini bonsai!
First, learn the basics, then once you've got the hang of
things, try out different compositions. After making one
super-mini bonsai, you're sure to want to make more.

Deutzia

Japanese maple

Cotoneaster

How to Make Super-mini Bonsai

Here, I'm making a super-mini bonsai from a Japanese box cutting. Understanding how to prepare and plant a seedling or cutting and how to use sphagnum moss and other mosses form the basis of making and repotting super-mini bonsai.

Japanese stewartia

Cedar

Andromeda

Rockspray cotoneaster

Neaten the plant

Remove dead or damaged leaves as well as unnecessary leaves at the lower end of the stalk to neaten the cutting or seedling.

TIDBIT

What should I do with the roots when repotting?

When repotting at the optimal time (March), trees are dormant so it's fine to cut the roots, but if repotting at other times, avoid cutting the roots as much as possible to lessen the damage to the tree.

If it's impossible to avoid cutting the roots, remove the same amount of leaves from the tree to maintain balance.

Match the plant and the pot

Check whether the plant complements the pot and whether it will look attractive once planted.

Test the position the plant in the pot to see whether it looks balanced. The plant can be positioned in the center or towards the edge of the pot.

Add soil

Add a spoonful of soil. Start off by adding enough to lightly cover the base of the pot.

Plant the cutting/seedling

Carefully pace the plant in the pot from the tips of the roots, making sure not to damage them.

Keeping what will become the front of the plant and pot in mind to create good balance, secure the plant in the pot.

TIDBIT

Where is the "front" of a tree?

There is a definite outer and inner side to each tree. Consider a Japanese garden—many rooms built for viewing gardens are south facing. Trees grow the most leaves on the south side, which gets the most sun, so the side of the tree viewed from the room is the one with fewer leaves.

In other words, the side with fewer leaves is the outer side or front of the tree. However, when making super-mini bonsai there's no need to worry too much about this as long as it looks attractive when planted!

● Add more soil

Hold the plant in place as you add soil.

Use tweezers to push soil into gaps between the roots.

TIP

Pack soil in firmly. If there is too little soil, the plant will not be stable and may easily fall over, so when starting the process, it's OK to add soil to the point of overflowing. Use the tweezers to push soil in between roots and pack it down firmly.

● Add soil again to stabilize

Add more soil, using tweezers to push soil in and fill gaps.

Use tweezers to push soil in.

Repeat the step of adding soil and pushing it into place with tweezers several times until the soil is packed in to a level just below the rim of the pot.

● Spread sphagnum moss over soil

Shred a small amount of sphagnum moss and soak it in water to prepare it.

Lay it on top of the soil.

TIP

Sphagnum moss acts as a "lid" on the soil. As well as preventing soil from spilling out or being blown away in the wind, sphagnum moss spread on top of the soil acts to lessen the degree to which soil dries out. Insufficient sphagnum moss is ineffective, while too much repels water, so use just enough to cover the soil.

Prepare moss and use tweezers to pinch off a little at a time.

Use tweezers to lightly push into sphagnum moss and gently plant moss in.

In the same way, plant moss in two other spots in the pot, keeping overall balance in mind.

● Water in

Carefully place the super-mini bonsai in a bucket or container full of water. Leave it there for about 10 seconds, until bubbles have stopped appearing.

● Done

In order for the plant to take to the soil and stabilize, place in a semi-shaded spot for about a week to 10 days after planting and water every day, monitoring the condition.

TIDBIT

Where should the tree be positioned in the pot?

In order for the roots to spread out equally inside the pot and ensure that the super-mini bonsai lasts for a long time, it's best to position the tree in the center of the pot. However, shaping the tree your own way, such as setting the trunk on a diagonal angle, is one of the joys of bonsai too. To angle the trunk diagonally, position the tree at the edge of the pot. Once you get the hang of super-mini bonsai, visualize the end result and have a go at various ways of planting.

To grow the trunk on an angle, plant the tree so that the roots are at the side of the pot.

Snowbell (Styrax obassia)

Creating a Super-mini Bonsai with a Twisted Trunk

"Twisted super-mini bonsai" are bonsai whose trunks have been wound around a bamboo skewer to give them a twisted look. Authentic bonsai are kept in place with wire and take years to achieve this kind of form, but super-mini bonsai allow this charming shape to be completed in a short time.

Cotoneaster (left) and Japanese maple (right).

Akebiae

Ring-cupped oak (Quercus glauca)

TIDBIT

Trees suitable for "twisted super-mini bonsai"

The shape of twisted super-mini bonsai is created by winding their trunks around bamboo skewers. Select trees that are still young and have long, thin trunks. Here, I've used a two-year-old Chinese fringe tree. You can also use Japanese maples, Japanese black pines and so on.

Choose fine, pliable wire

When making super-mini bonsai, use fine, pliable wire that won't damage the thin trunk of the tree, such as 0.8mm aluminum wire. It's not expensive, but few places stock it in the small quantities used for bonsai making, so it may be difficult to find. Try looking at gardening stores that stock super-mini bonsai.

● Prepare the plant and bamboo skewer

TIP

How to wind is up to you.
Where you start and finish winding is up to personal taste. Wind as few or as many times as you like, or position the skewer on an angle to achieve the various forms in the pictures on page 30.

Line up the trunk of the plant against the skewer and consider the desired result.

Strip the dead or extraneous leaves from the plant to neaten its appearance.

● Secure the start of the winding with wire

Attach the tip of the skewer just below the area to be wound.

Wind wire around the trunk and skewer about three times to secure.

The wire wound around to secure the trunk to the skewer. Cut off excess wire with pliers.

● Wind trunk around skewer

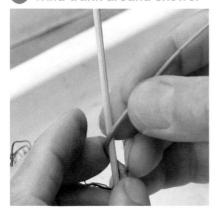

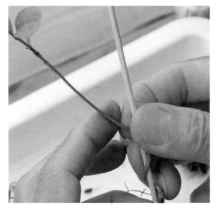

Starting from the section secured with wire and working up, wind the trunk around the skewer.

Wind carefully to prevent snapping or damaging the trunk.

TIP

Wind reasonably firmly.
To achieve a neatly twisted trunk, wind trunk slightly firmly and with only short gaps between windings around the skewer.

● Keep winding

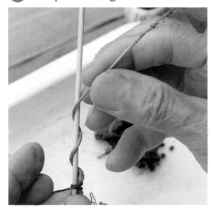

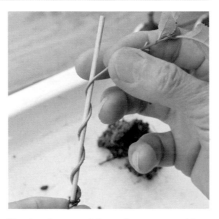

Twist
Twist

Picture the end result as you keep winding.

The trunk wound three times around the skewer. In this example, this concludes the winding.

● Secure the end of the winding

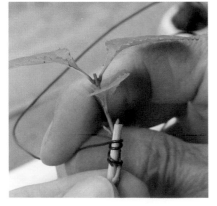

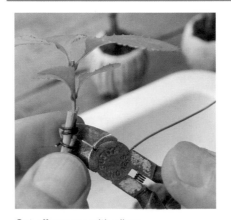

Wind wire around the end of the winding about three times to secure the trunk to the skewer.

Cut off excess with pliers.

The finished result with the trunk wound around the skewer. The tree will be planted as it is.

● Plant in pot

Match the plant and the pot for balance and decide where the front of the bonsai will be.

Add soil to pot and plant tree.

TIP

Plant as per the basics!
Planting the tree, laying sphagnum moss over the soil, adding moss and finally watering the bonsai are the steps that remain basically unchanged for any super-mini bonsai. Familiarize yourself with the basics from pages 27–29.

Add soil until the plant is stable and secure.

● Apply sphagnum moss

Shred a small amount of sphagnum moss and soak it in water before laying it on top of the soil.

TIDBIT

When and how should the wire and skewer be removed?

A tree trunk wound around a bamboo skewer will thicken and harden a little in about a year as it grows in the twisted shape. If left in place, the wire will damage the tree as it continues to grow, so remove it after a year.

To remove the wire, cut through it with pliers and pull out the skewer.

● Apply moss

Use tweezers to plant moss in three places in the sphagnum moss.

● Done

After soaking the entire pot in a bucket of water, allow the plant and soil to stabilize for a week to 10 days in a semi-shaded spot, monitoring the condition.

Wound-round Super-mini Bonsai

"Wound-round" super-mini bonsai are bonsai with their trunks wound around and around like a Christmas wreath. They can be created from creeping plants that are close to hand.

Ficus thunbergii (two years old)

Ficus thunbergii (three years old)

Ficus thunbergii (one year old)

TIDBIT

Plants suitable for wound-round super-mini bonsai

Creeping plants such as those which grow on the walls of houses or along fences are suitable for these kinds of super-mini bonsai.

Vines and creepers put out roots from their stems—whichever section of stem is planted in the ground, it will grow roots. Further, they are always putting out roots and can be used just as they are immediately after being harvested, so there is no need to grow them from cuttings.

In this example, Ficus thunbergii has been used, but plants such as ivy and spindle trees that are familiar as ornamental and garden plants can be used in the same way.

Choose plants with pliable, supple trunks that won't break regardless of how much they are bent.

Decide on the starting point

Visualize which part of the plant to show and how big to make the loop.

Wind one round and make the starting point where the form is well-balanced.

Wind wind

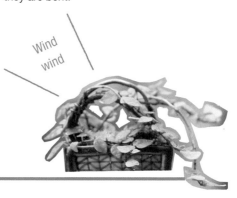

Secure the start of the loop with wire

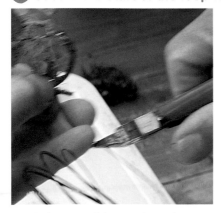

Wind wire around the starting point about three times and cut off excess with pliers.

The vine wound in a loop. Remove the excess leaves from the lower section.

TIP

The starting point is the part that gets planted. Secured with wire, the section with the starting point will eventually be planted at the base of the pot, with the upper half of the loop visible above the soil. Keep this in mind and work to achieve overall balance.

Creating a "Seed-showing" Super-mini Bonsai

I've called these examples "seed-showing" super-mini bonsai as they are grown from seeds and acorns which lie above the soil and form part of the composition. These uniquely-shaped plants showcase the possibilities of super-mini bonsai.

Chinese fringe tree

Ring-cupped oak (Quercus glauca)

Sawtooth oak

You will need

- A seedling with the seed still attached (see page 24)
- Pot
- Soil
- Sphagnum moss
- Moss

Tools

- Scissors
- Tweezers
- Wire (aluminum wire 1.0 mm thick)
- Wire cutting pliers
- Small spoon (to fill pot with soil)
- Bucket (large enough to hold plenty of water)

TIDBIT

Exposed root bonsai—a hit in the bonsai world

The super-mini bonsai being made in this example shows the seed from which it grew and is also a *ne-agari* or exposed root bonsai, meaning that the tree's roots are exposed above the ground. Ne-agari bonsai resemble trees that grow in coastal areas or the sides of cliffs and have been tossed about by wind and rain. Exposing the twisted roots above the level of the soil to look like the trunk allows the tree's various transformations to be enjoyed.

The twisted section of this tree is actually the root. Exposing the roots allows interesting shapes to form.

Decide on the starting point for the exposed root

Look carefully at the seedling to decide where to make the starting point for the exposed root (the point between the above-ground and below-ground section of the root).

Wrap wire around the starting point.

TIP

Leave a length of wire below the starting point. The wire will be used to secure the plant into the pot, so make sure to leave it long.

Exposed seed

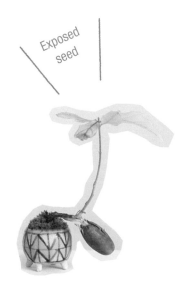

Start winding wire around the root

Wrap wire around the root.

Wrap wire around root, twisting the wire and root as you go to create shape.

● Wind wire around the trunk

As for the root, wind wire around the section of trunk above the seed.

Finish winding a little below the leaf.

Secure wire to finish winding and trim off excess wire with pliers.

● Create shape

The root and trunk wrapped in wire.

Bend the wire-bound root and trunk to create shape.

TIP

An eye for shape. How you bend the tree is up to you. However, if the center of balance is off, the pot will fall over, so keep this in mind when shaping the tree.

● Place in pot

The shaped seedling. Plant into the pot, starting by inserting the piece of wire left over from the start of the wrapping.

Pass wire through the hole in the base of the pot.

After passing wire through the hole, position plant to check whether it balances well with the pot.

Use wire to secure plant in pot

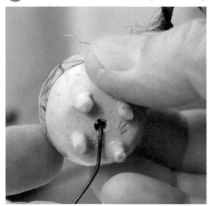

Wind wire protruding from the base around the pot.

Secure the shaped seedling into the pot so it can't move around.

Trim off excess wire with pliers and bend the end over the rim of the pot.

Plant in

Add soil and press in with tweezers until the soil is packed in to just below the rim of the pot.

Apply sphagnum moss

Shred a small amount of sphagnum moss and soak it in water before laying it on top of the soil.

Add moss

Use tweezers to plant moss in three places in the sphagnum moss.

Done

Water. Then, in order for the plant to take to the soil and stabilize, place in a semi-shaded spot for about a week to 10 days after planting, monitoring the condition.

TIDBIT

Don't allow the root to dry out

As the root is originally meant to be in the ground, it dries out more easily than the trunk and care must be taken with watering. At times when it is prone to drying out, it's a good idea to enclose it in a plastic bag.

Water the super-mini bonsai and seal it in a plastic bag placed in a cool spot.

Open the bag after 2–3 days and leave for a while to release humidity.

Fun with Composition

The "twisted trunk," "wound-round" and "seed-showing" variations introduced in Chapter 2 show how super-mini bonsai lend themselves to all kinds of compositions. Have fun with the endless design arrangements that super-mini bonsai make possible.

Is it OK to use seeds from consumed fruit to grow super-mini bonsai?

The appeal of super-mini bonsai is that they allow the grower to easily experience all the charm of traditional bonsai. At the same time, super-mini bonsai offer a new way to enjoy the art of bonsai, so there are no hard-and-fast rules that must be followed, and part of their appeal lies in challenging the taboos of traditional bonsai.

For instance, one way to create super-mini bonsai is to grow the plant from seed. There's no need to buy any special seeds—experiment by using the seeds of avocados, mangos and so on that have been enjoyed. You may not know what kind of shoots to expect or whether the plant will grow to maturity, but super-mini bonsai allow you to have fun experimenting. Have a go at creating an original world—one that is beautiful to you—inside a little pot.

SUPER-MINI BONSAI COMPOSITION 1

Group planting

In traditional bonsai, it's accepted that group plantings are of the same species, but in this example, various types are grouped together to resemble a dense forest and create overall visual appeal.

At front/left are one-year-old silk trees, while two-year-old Japanese cypresses are at the back/right.

SUPER-MINI BONSAI COMPOSITION 2

A pine cone as a design accent

A pine cone can be used as a source of seeds to grow seedlings, but here it also forms a decoration. The pine seedling has been planted at the edge of the pot with the pine cone boldly worked in to the composition.

Over time, the pine cone will gain character, lending an artistic touch.

Chapter 3

Super-mini Bonsai Maintenance

The most important thing to consider when growing super-mini bonsai is watering. Additionally, if the branches are cared for and the plant is regularly repotted, it can last for years, and its development and changing appearance will be a source of pleasure. So make sure you have a firm grasp of the fundamentals of maintenance.

Variegated spindle tree

Orostachys japonica [aka rock pine]
(lotus nail)

Japanese maple

Fundamentals for Regular Care

To keep a super-mini bonsai healthy over a long period of time, daily watering is necessary, along with regular fertilizing, disinfection and pest control. Occasionally, observe it carefully up close to take note of any changes.

Place in a sunny, airy spot

Apart from when they are on display inside, super-mini bonsai should be kept outdoors. Because of their small size they can be grown on a balcony just as well as in a garden. For robust growth, in spring and fall they should receive 2–3 hours of sunlight and fresh air each day. A suitable spot for this may not come to mind straight away, but conditions can be improved with some adjustments. Find a way to make your surroundings work for you.

CHOOSING THE RIGHT LOCATION

Ensure that sunlight and air are adequate
Placed on a shelf with space in between them, super-mini bonsai will receive plenty of sunshine and improved air flow. If you don't have an actual shelf, place a plank over some bricks or use a wooden crate instead. Placing bonsai on wood is preferable to metal or concrete as wood moderates the effects of heat and cold.

Do not place directly on the ground
If placed in direct contact with the ground, bonsai may be affected by harmful insects getting into the pot or by mud splashing in and spreading diseases. Take particular care not to place bonsai directly on concrete as the radiant heat can damage them.

Adjust care depending on the season, plant variety and so on

Super-mini bonsai are grown in little pots with only a small amount of soil, so their care requires a certain level of detail, especially in summer and winter. In summer, they must be shielded from strong sunlight and heat, while in winter measures such as covering them in plastic sheets at night must be taken to provide protection from the cold.

Maintenance requirements differ slightly depending on plant types. Different plants have different needs: some like shade, others like dry places and so on. We won't go into the characteristics of each plant here, but it's a good idea to refer to gardening books, magazines and websites to learn as much as you can about the plants you are growing.

 SPRING The gentle sunlight of spring makes it an easy season for growing bonsai. Stick to the basics of placing bonsai in a sunny spot outside. It is the season for new buds, which are very delicate. Take steps to ensure that plants are not blown over and damaged by the wind, such as positioning them near a wall.

 SUMMER Summer heat can cause soil to drain too readily and dry out. Drooping leaves are a telltale sign of dehydrated soil. Make sure to water properly twice a day. It's also important to place the bonsai in a spot with good air flow but out of direct sun. Covering the plant with cheesecloth or similar is an effective solution.

FALL As in spring, fall is a season when it's easy to grow things. Make sure plants get enough sunlight, and for some small trees in particular (see page 69), it's time to build up their store of nutrients before they shed their leaves in preparation for going into dormancy over winter. Give them some fertilizer and make appropriate preparations to protect them from the cold.

 WINTER Watch out for frost and freezing during winter. Small, delicate plants like these are susceptible to winter hazards. Fine branches can be burned by frost, and roots can become damaged if the soil in the pot freezes over. Cover these plants with plastic sheets or place them in a styrofoam box to insulate them against the cold. It's also important to move them to a covered area.

WATERING	As super-mini bonsai are planted in such a small amount of soil, water retention is poor and soil dries out rapidly. Therefore, watering is the most important aspect of maintenance.

Water thoroughly

It's not good to have either too little or too much moisture in the soil in the pot. If there is too little, the bonsai will not be able to develop properly, while too much moisture means the roots are constantly soaking in water, leading to root decay.

The frequency with which you water must be altered according to the season. A rough guideline is to water twice a day in summer; once a day in spring and fall and once every three days in winter. Use a watering can if you're growing bonsai outside, or soak them water if your space makes using a can awkward.

Either way, the key is to water thoroughly—to the extent that water is dripping from the base of the pot. It's important to get water flowing through the pot. Rather than giving a lot of water at once, water regularly to maintain appropriate moisture levels.

Moss acts as a barometer for watering

There is an obvious aesthetic reason for planting moss with bonsai, but moss also acts as a barometer for managing watering as it changes color and withers if it receives too little or too much water. Conversely, if it receives the right amount of water, sunlight and fresh air, it will be a healthy, luxuriant green. Moss growing well is a sign that you are watering properly.

Moss not only improves the appearance of bonsai, but also acts as a watering barometer.

USING A WATERING CAN

If growing bonsai outdoors, use a watering can to distribute moisture evenly. Rather than giving plants a lot of water all at once, water thoroughly by showering them a little at a time. When they have been watered once, wait a little while and water again, then wait and repeat once more to ensure they have received plenty of water.

SOAKING IN WATER

On balconies and in cramped places where it's hard to use a watering can, fill a container with water and soak plants instead. Gently submerge the entire pot until bubbles start appearing. Leave the pot in the water until the bubbles stop forming.

| **FERTILIZING** | In a pot, the room for the nutrients a plant requires is limited, so it is necessary to fertilize. As a guide, liquid fertilizer should be given twice a month and solid fertilizer twice a year. |

Different uses for liquid and solid fertilizers

There are liquid and solid fertilizers. Liquid fertilizers are compound fertilizers that are diluted in water, so are effective immediately. They last only a short time, so make sure to apply a light dilution often. When the plant is in its growth period, fertilize twice a month. Conversely, solid fertilizer is made from ingredients including oil meal and ground bone, and is continually effective over a long period. Apply it twice a year, in spring (around May) and fall (around September).

When there are no longer any nutrients in the soil, the color of a plant's leaves becomes lighter and shoots don't grow properly. Check the conditions of your bonsai regularly to make sure you don't miss any changes in their appearance.

APPLYING LIQUID FERTILIZER

Dilute liquid fertilizer to the volume prescribed on the label.

Use an oil can to apply as close to the base of the tree as possible.

APPLYING SOLID FERTILIZER

Fine-grained fertilizers that are used for vegetables, wild grasses and so on are suitable for super-mini bonsai.

Shake some solid fertilizer into your hand and pick up one grain with the tweezers.

Make a hole in the sphagnum moss with the tweezers and press fertilizer in. Do this in about two places per pot.

KILLING PESTS AND DISINFECTING

As super-mini bonsai are so small, if they are infested by insects the damage done is much greater than to that of a regular bonsai. Take firm steps to prevent this happening.

A sunny, airy spot makes for healthy plants

The best way to protect plants from insects damage is to keep them robust. Place them in a spot that is suitable for their development, with plenty of sunshine and fresh air, and make sure they get enough water and fertilizer for healthy growth. When repotting, check the backs of leaves for harmful insects.

In addition, make sure to disinfect the plants and apply pesticide. Disinfection and pesticide application should be carried out about once a month as a preventative measure against harmful pests that attack the plant during its grown period.

DISINFECTING AND APPLYING PESTICIDE

Japanese brands of spreading agent (used to mix with pesticide and fungicide to ensure even application to the plant) pesticide (to kill harmful insects); fungicide (to kill microbes). **When buying these products, choose the safest, most natural and bonsai-friendly brands you can find.**

Mix the three agents in a spray bottle to apply over plants.

COMMON PESTS AND HOW TO DEAL WITH THEM

PEST	SYMPTOMS	TREATMENT
Powdery mildew	The backs of the leaves are covered in white mold, appearing as if they have been smeared with flour.	Prevent the condition by placing plant in a sunny spot with good air flow. If it occurs, apply a solution of anti-mildew agent.
Sooty mold	Branches, leaves and the surface of the trunk appear to be covered with soot. This is caused by mold which lives on the excrement of aphids and other pest insects.	Applying an agent to kill pest insects will prevent this condition.
Leaf spot disease	Small brown spots appear on the leaves, causing them to change color. This is commonly caused by mold.	If spots appear, remove the affected leaves and apply a solution to treat the condition.
Aphids	Starting with new buds on small trees, these insects infest the entire plant, consuming the sap and impeding the development of the tree.	If an infestation occurs, use a brush to lightly knock off insects and apply an appropriate solution.
Mites	Mites break out on the backs of leaves and consume the sap. White spots appear on the fronts of leaves and the leaves lose their color.	Mites thrive in high temperatures and dry conditions, so wet the backs of the leaves. If an outbreak occurs, apply an appropriate solution.
Scale insect	These insects appear on bark and stalks, sucking the tree's sap.	Use a brush to lightly knock off insects and apply an appropriate solution.

BRANCH MAINTENANCE

In order for trees to develop properly and keep their shape, it's necessary to trim off sections from overgrown branches. This is known as pruning.

Keep the desired shape in mind as you neaten branches

One of the purposes of pruning is to keep the tree growing healthily. Trimming off extraneous branches or branches that have got too big and placing the plant in a spot that gets plenty of sun and fresh air makes it easy for the tree to develop and prevents infestations and damage by pest insects.

Another reason to prune is to maintain the overall form and size of the tree. Keep in mind the shape to be maintained and neaten the form by removing protruding branches. Pruning also encourages blossoming and fruiting, so it is an important task.

The best time to prune depends on the type of tree, but in general, just before spring when new buds are forming is a good time to prune small trees, while pinales should be pruned in the period from late fall to early spring and flowering trees should be pruned after blossoming. Further, pruning should be guided by the growth of the tree, so trim branches off if they are getting too long.

HOW TO PRUNE

With the image of the future form in mind, check for overgrown or extraneous branches.

Leaving individual branches that you wish to grow, use pruning scissors to trim off other branches at their bases.

A super-mini bonsai neatened after pruning, and the trimmed branches. It's a good idea to grow these as they can be used as cuttings.

Daily maintenance keeps a tree robust for formation of flower buds

In order to achieve blossoms, it's necessary to understand how each tree forms flower buds to allow for flower differentiation, the process by which flowers are formed. For flower differentiation to occur, the tree must have sufficient stores of strength from plenty of sunlight and fertilizer, so first of all, ensure regular maintenance. Many trees form flower buds in summer, so make sure not to cut branches after early summer. Any branches that grow after early summer will not form flower buds. Further, trees draw nutrients from their leaves in order to form flower buds, so make sure they are free of insect damage.

To ensure flowering the following year also, remove the flower husks before fruit has formed. Blossoming uses up a lot of the tree's strength, so make sure to fertilize and water thoroughly after the tree has finished flowering.

A flowering crab apple in bloom. Flowering (ornamental) cherries, plums and weeping forsythia also make good flowering trees.

Keep water off flowers to achieve fruit

In order for a tree to achieve fruit it must first bud and flower. As per achieving blossoms, it is important first of all to ensure the tree's overall health through regular care and maintenance. To achieve fruit, water the tree at the roots, since watering the flowers can hinder pollination. How fruit develops depends on the type of tree. Some trees have flowers with stamens and pistils inside the same flower which pollinate after blossoming and then form fruit (such as crab apples), while on other trees such as the Japanese spindle tree, flowers with stamens and flowers with pistils blossom on separate trees so both trees are needed for pollination to occur.

Once a tree has fruited and you have admired it for a while, remove the fruit as soon as possible to lessen the burden on the tree.

A flowering crab apple bearing fruit. Other recommended fruiting trees include crab apples and fire thorns.

| Just as branches are neatened through pruning, roots should be tidied up too. Repotting is necessary for keeping the tree healthy over a long period.

Refresh soil to stimulate root growth

As bonsai develop, their roots grow to fill the whole pot. If left like this, a lack of oxygen will prevent roots growing any further, so it's necessary to remove the entire plant from the pot, treat the roots and change the soil.

When repotting, when you've removed tree to trim overgrown and extraneous roots, also replace the old soil. This is necessary because as time passes, individual grains of soil break down and clump together, making it difficult for water and air to pass through. Further, elements in the soil such as nitrogen, phosphate and potassium are essential for a tree's development, but these become depleted over time. It's necessary to refresh the soil in order to replace these elements.

March—before plants' active growth period—is the best time for repotting

The best time for repotting varies depending on the type of plant, but in general March is suitable as it is before the active growth period in spring, when plants put out new shoots. Rather than during the extreme temperatures of mid-summer or mid-winter, repotting is best carried out during the more moderate weather in spring and fall. If repotted in spring, the roots of plants such as roses and quinces will be damaged, so they must be repotted in fall.

Repotting and tidying up the roots will reduce the number of delicate roots that transport water up the plant and consequently lessen the plant's ability to absorb water. Make sure to give the plant plenty of water well before it dries out.

Water not soaking into the pot properly is a sign that the roots have become too dense and repotting is required.

TIDBIT

Other plants need repotting too

Just as you would repot plants which have been made into super-mini bonsai, it is necessary to repot other pot-bound plants once a year. The method is the same as for super-mini bonsai—tidy up the roots and refresh the soil.

Remove the entire plant and soil to repot.

1 Remove super-mini bonsai, soil, moss and sphagnum moss from pot.

2 Use tweezers to gently brush off soil around the roots. When repotting super-mini bonsai, remove all old soil and replace it with new soil.

3 Use scissors to trim off roots all around. Take off about 1/3 of what was originally there.

4 Follow the same steps involved in the basics of making super-mini bonsai (pages 26–29) to fill the pot with new soil, plant in the bonsai and cover the soil with sphagnum moss and moss.

Proper regular maintenance lets you enjoy bonsai for a long time

Although they are small, with daily watering and regular fertilizing and pest prevention, super-mini bonsai will grow healthily, and with repotting, can live for years in a little pot. Putting some effort into them will allow you to enjoy their calming presence for a long time.

Pruning maintains the shape and size of the super-mini bonsai, but even if their size doesn't alter much, the plant changes with the passing of time. Leaves change color, flowers blossom, fruit forms—and apart from these seasonal changes, the tree's trunk strengthens, its form becomes more defined and its character emerges. Super-mini bonsai allow you to view nature's image inside a little pot. Try working a little bit of nature into your lifestyle.

One-year-old pine super-mini bonsai.

Two-year-old pine super-mini bonsai.

When You're Away for a Few Days

When the whole family goes on holiday or those who live alone have to be away for a while, keep these points in mind for how to treat super-mini bonsai.

Preventing dehydration is paramount

You may think it's difficult to go on vacation while growing bonsai, but not so. With proper preparation, bonsai can be left for a week in midsummer and up to two weeks in winter with no problems.

The most important thing is to set up the pot so that it does not dry out. The conditions that cause the pot to dry out are 1. high temperatures 2. low humidity and 3. good air flow, so make sure these do not occur simultaneously. The most effective means of doing this is by sealing the bonsai into a plastic bag or lidded container. For absences of two or three days, the super-mini bonsai can be watered and placed in a tray in the bathroom or shower room with the door shut.

METHOD OF CARE DURING AN ABSENCE 1

Seal in a plastic bag

Water the bonsai and enclose it in a plastic bag, then place it in the bathroom or other spot that is cool and away from sun. This is important especially in summer to avoid too much heat and humidity.

Sealing the bonsai in a plastic bag is the easiest and most effective method.

METHOD OF CARE DURING AN ABSENCE 2

Seal in a container with damp newspaper

Another method is to place the super-mini bonsai in a container with wet, lightly wrung newspaper. If placed in the container so it can't move, it's possible to carry the super-mini bonsai around over short distances.

Water the super-mini bonsai on top of damp newspaper inside a container.

Close the lid so the container won't dry out.

Chapter 4

Displaying and Enjoying Super-mini Bonsai

Once you've created your super-mini bonsai, be sure to display it as you would a piece of stylish decor. Simply placing a little bonsai in a space lends it a sense of calm warmth. Try it when you invite friends to visit.

Rockspray cotoneaster

Ivy

Variegated spindle tree
(Euonymus fortunei)

A white ceramic trivet forms a "little island" on the tabletop, decorated with super-mini bonsai and pebbles.

Create and Enjoy a Little World

Do you love looking at miniature dolls and animals, little knick knacks and small bits of nature? Create a special world in miniature with super-mini bonsai, imagining all kinds of stories as you go.

A super-mini bonsai and tiny hedgehog look like they are having a conversation. Don't the trunk and leaves look as if they're leaning in to listen?

A wooden box, handkerchief and cardboard boxes are combined in dollhouse style. I chose the red handkerchief to add an accent color.

Display with Your Favorite Knick Knacks

Sweet little super-mini bonsai can be displayed just as if they were knick knacks. They suit both Japanese and western-style interiors, so display them to match your décor.

Postcards are just the right size to perfectly complement super-mini bonsai in a display. Puzzling about how to showcase them is an enjoyable pastime.

A single super-mini bonsai stands with a collection of glass items on a display shelf. The pink flower forms an eye-catching accent.

Easy Ways to Work Super-mini Bonsai Into Your Daily Life

When bonsai are at their best, with dense foliage, flowers blooming or fruit ripening, have them at your side to enjoy. Your everyday living space will transform into something a little bit special.

Super-mini bonsai casually displayed alongside everyday items in a kitchen or bathroom bring color to a living space. Although small, their presence shines.

A well-formed super-mini bonsai placed on a book shelf. Ornamental plants and cut flowers are great, but super-mini bonsai are truly refined.

When displaying indoors, little plates and dishes are extremely useful as saucers.
Try sitting super-mini bonsai on various little plates placed all around a room.

Being able to see super-mini bonsai from the corner of your eye while you're working on your computer is relaxing. If you use a box or something to display them, you won't accidentally knock them over.

A Place of Calm in a Room

The busier or more stressed you are, the more even a tiny thing can help you relax. Simply having a little bonsai in the room makes the atmosphere calmer.

A calendar featuring photos of plants works with the real thing. The rich variety of color and shape in the pots makes for an interesting space.

Give Displays an Authentic Touch

There are various rules for displaying traditional bonsai. Here are some ways specialist bonsai accessories can lend authenticity to methods of displaying super-mini bonsai.

Use accessories such as display stands to showcase bonsai in alcoves, on shelves and so on

Broadly speaking, there are two ways to display bonsai. One of these is called *toko-kazari* and involves displaying bonsai in an alcove (the "*toko-noma*" used to display objects in Japanese homes). It is usual for these displays to comprise a "main" tree and an "attendant" tree, and they may also be combined with a hanging scroll.

The other way is *tana-kazari* and involves placing a display shelf with multiple bonsai on it in an alcove. Many regular small bonsai are shown in this manner, with groupings conventionally always in odd numbers of three, five or seven. Fundamental to both of these display methods is the use of a platform (*taku*) or board (*jiita*) beneath the bonsai.

Seasonal and natural scenery expressed in a miniature world

Bonsai express seasonal and natural scenery inside their own little world. For instance, they can be made to resemble the scenery of mountains and valleys or express the changing of the four seasons, with the overall display creating a world view.

Particularly when displaying several small bonsai together, their combination and the space around them is important. Rather than simply being lined up next to one another, it's the drawing out of depth and height that create a world of refinement and dignity.

Super-mini bonsai appeal because they can be shown freely in a contemporary style, but incorporating traditional methods into their display allows them to be appreciated in yet another way.

TRADITIONAL DISPLAY EXAMPLE

Use stands and boards for authenticity

The platform in the center back is called a *taku* (stand), the board placed under the bonsai at the front is a *jiita* and the shelf holding multiple super-mini bonsai is called a *kazari*. Many bonsai display items are readily available. Mame-bonsai displays are great for super-mini bonsai. From right to left, the seven bonsai in this picture represent spring, summer, fall and winter.

The key to a great display is careful attention to overall balance, such as the straight growth of a trunk, the angle of another, the density of foliage and so on.

Chapter 5

All Kinds of Super-mini Bonsai

Although super-mini bonsai are small, they are just like real bonsai in that they allow various types and shapes of tree to be enjoyed. This chapter will help you brush up on the basics of bonsai tree types and forms in order to better understand bonsai and fully appreciate their charm.

Japanese white pine
(Pinus parviflora)

Red chokeberry

Juneberry
(Amelanchier canadensis)

Types of Bonsai

The single word "bonsai" encompasses many types of tree. Understanding the various characteristics and deepening your knowledge of each tree type will make it easier to grow bonsai in line with your expectations.

Dividing bonsai into four broad categories

Bonsai are broadly divided into four tree types: pinales, small trees, flowering trees and fruiting trees. Generally, pines and other trees which are strongly associated with bonsai fall into the pinale category. Trees other than pinales are "small trees." Apart from these, there are trees which are appreciated for their flowers or fruit.

TREE TYPE 1 **PINALES**

Conifers: the best known bonsai

Pines, cedars, Chinese junipers and their ilk are evergreen conifers. As shaping them requires a degree of technique, they are generally suited to intermediate to advanced bonsai practitioners, but their established role as the face of bonsai lends them a high status with much appeal. They are robust and live long. When growing these as super-mini bonsai, gather the seeds from pine cones and grow seedlings.

> **TYPICAL PINALES**
> Japanese red pine (Pinus densiflora),
> Japanese black pine (Pinus thunbergii),
> cedar, Japanese cypress, Chinese juniper

Japanese white pine (Pinus parviflora)

Deciduous trees other than Pinales

Trees other than Pinales are grouped together as "small trees." Most are deciduous, with their appeal lying in their changing form and leaf color: they bud in spring, put forth new foliage in early summer, change color in fall and drop their leaves in winter. There are various types which are easy to grow and lend themselves to shaping, making them ideal for beginners.

TYPICAL SMALL TREE
Japanese maple, zelkova, beech, hornbeam, tall stewartia, ivy

Trident maple

Grape

TIDBIT

Non-woody perennials shaped as bonsai

Apart from bonsai made from trees, there are also non-woody bonsai which are made from perennial flowering plants. These non-woody bonsai have a charming simplicity and sweetness. They can be made using one type of flowering plant, and are also attractive when grouped.

A prettily flowering azure bluet (Houstonia caerulea) made into a super-mini bonsai.

Flowering bonsai put on a splendid show

These trees are grown for their flowers, and when in bloom they delight with their air of splendor. To ensure that the flowers bloom, do some research in advance to find out when flower buds will form so that you don't cut them off. Flowering uses up the tree's energy, so remember to thank it by applying fertilizer to replenish its strength.

TYPICAL FLOWERING TREES
Plum, ornamental cherry,
flowering crab apple, Deutzia,
Japanese stewartia

Flowering crab apple

Japanese bladdernut (Staphylia)

Lonicera gracilipes (honeysuckle)

Fire thorn

Fruiting bonsai capture fall tastes

There is a wealth of varieties of trees that can
be grown for their show of fruit. In order for
fruit to form, cross-fertilization is necessary.
There are various ways for this to occur, such
as monoecious (self) pollination, pollination
requiring a partner (dioecious pollination) and
hermaphroditic pollination. It's important to
know how to look after the tree once it has
finished fruiting as its strength will be depleted.

Hawthorn

Rockspray cotoneaster

TYPICAL FRUITING TREES
Fire thorn, hawthorn, crab apple,
Japanese winterberry

Enjoy the Differences in Tree Form

Tree form describes a tree's figure and shape. There are basic forms for bonsai that have become established over the art's long history. The tree forms of super-mini bonsai can be appreciated just as are those of larger bonsai.

Creating tree form—one of bonsai's greatest pleasures

The difference between bonsai and other pot plants and decorative plants is that bonsai's branches, leaves and so on are manipulated for ornamental purposes. In other words, it can be said that the greatest enjoyment in the art of bonsai is creating their form.

Tree forms are modeled on those found in nature. In order to achieve this expression in a small pot, wire is wrapped around the trunk, branches are pruned and much time is spent in their creation.

The forms shown here are popular with many people and have become established as "beautiful" over bonsai's long history. The same forms can be recreated in super-mini bonsai—in fact, forms that take several years to achieve in bigger bonsai can be created in a short amount of time such as half a year to a year in super-mini bonsai. They allow even beginners to experience and enjoy bonsai's charm—that is, shaping the tree.

Once you know the basics of tree form, it becomes easier to achieve the image you have in mind. Pay a visit to bonsai exhibitions and fairs to see bonsai for yourself and pick up some ideas.

TREE FORM 1 **STRAIGHT TRUNK** •

Acer palmatum matsumurae

An excellent choice for evoking a landscape

In this form, a single trunk firmly rooted into the ground stretches skyward. Like a big, solitary tree rising from the top of a hill, it makes a powerful, stately impression. To create this form, choose a type of tree that grows with a straight trunk such as a pine, cedar or other tree from the Pinales family, or a small tree such as a zelkova, and correct the shape so it doesn't bend by wrapping with wire and pruning. It's usual to shape the tree so the upper branches are narrower.

> **TREE TYPES SUITED TO STRAIGHT TRUNK FORMS**
> Pine, cedar, zelkova etc

A fun challenge in creating balance

This form refers to trees with trunks leaning to the left or right and replicates the form of trees found in nature which grow towards the sun. As super-mini bonsai are in small pots, bad overall balance causes them to tip over easily, so create stability by positioning the tree base at the edge of the pot and allowing the leaves to grow densely all around.

> **TREE TYPES SUITED TO ANGLED TRUNK FORMS**
> Any type of tree is OK

Cotoneaster

Silver lacevine

Blueberry

TIDBIT

When should I remove the wire?

When creating tree forms, you may wonder about the timing for removing wire from trees that are being shaped. Remove the wire from the top part of the branch and lightly touch it. If it doesn't shift into a different shape, it means the form is completed and the wire can be removed.

If wire is left wrapped around a tree without ever being removed, it will eat into the branch and leave a scar. It is not easy to get rid of marks on branches, so make sure to regularly check wire in order to avoid scarring.

One tree divided into two at the base

In this form, the tree is divided into two different sized trunks at the base. It's usual to make one trunk large and the other small, with the large one known as the principal trunk and the small one as the deputy trunk. The form closely recalls a parent and child nestling together. If the two trunks are leaning in different directions it will look as if there is something missing in between, so both trunks growing in the same direction is the preferred form.

TREES SUITED TO TWIN-TRUNK FORMS
Any type of tree is OK

Spindle tree
(Euonymus fortunei)

One tree divided into three at the base

In contrast with the twin-trunk form which is divided into two, this form is divided into three. As per the twin-trunk form, each trunk in the three-trunk form is made different in terms of size, volume of foliage and so on.

When shaping the tree, use wire to correct the three trunks so they are all leaning in the same direction.

Trident maple

TREES SUITED TO TREE-TRUNK FORMS
Any type of tree is OK

Multiple trunks growing from a single base

In contrast with twin-trunk and three-trunk forms, the clump form has five or more separate trunks growing from the base. The tallest and thickest is the principal trunk, while the other are known as branch trunks. The key to creating this form lies in striking the right balance between the trunks. The build-up of multiple trunks creates a form evocative of a thicket.

TREES SUITED TO CLUMP FORMS
Any type of tree is OK

Princess pussy willow

A thick trunk and branches that wind as they grow

In this form, the trunk and branches wind all around and the thick trunk becomes more and more tapered with height. The winding trunk is called the "bend." This is one of the most popular bonsai tree forms. While emphasizing the natural curves of the plant, the tree is pruned and corrected with wire to achieve the desired form over time.

TREES SUITED TO INFORMAL UPRIGHT FORMS
Japanese maple, camellia, pine etc

Oleaster

Chinese cork oak

Silverthorn (Eleagnus pungens)

A form flowing in one direction

In this form, the trunk and branches all flow in one direction as if bending before the wind. It expresses the vitality of strong, supple trees that grow on mountain sides and coastlines, buffeted by strong winds.

Trees with slender trunks suit this form, with fine trunks and branch tips stretching in all directions, giving off a feeling of vibrancy.

TREES SUITED TO WINDSWEPT FORMS

Pine, Japanese maple etc

Acer palmatum matsumurae

Miyama crab apple

A form resembling a tree cascading over a cliff

In this form, the trunk and branches spill out to hang lower than the pot itself. Bonsai that hang at about the same level as the rim of the pot are said to be in the semi-cascade style.

The cascade form is created in the image of vigorously growing trees clinging closely to precipitous cliff faces. If the bonsai is not balanced well, it can easily be tipped over, so rather than training the tree to grow in one direction, leave some branches and leaves growing in the opposite direction to the cascading section.

TREES SUITED TO CASCADE FORMS Pine, Chinese juniper etc

Create scenery with five or more trees

This form is created by planting multiple trees in single pot to create the appearance of a wood or forest.

The forest form involves planting several trees of various sizes, grouping their bases together and keeping overall balance in mind. The usual convention is to plant in odd numbers, such as five or seven.

TREES SUITED TO FOREST FORMS
Zelkova, beech, maple

Japanese maple

SUPER-MINI BONSAI GLOSSARY

Here, simple explanations are given for specialist words and terms relating to bonsai. Please make use of this list as a reference and to further your enjoyment of super-mini bonsai.

ACTIVE PERIOD (OR GROWTH PERIOD)
A period in which a plant blossoms, fruits, develops and grows vigorously.

ANGLED TRUNK
A bonsai tree form in which the trunk leans to one side.

ATTENDANT
A bonsai displayed to bring out the beauty of a principal tree. Can also describe a decorative object.

AXILLARY BUD
A bud that grows at the intersection of a branch and the trunk of a tree.

BEND
This describes the way in which a trunk or branches are bending. Correcting trees with wire to shape them is called "bending."

BUD PICKING
Trimming off of overgrown shoots with the aim of stimulating a second flush of growth.

CASCADE
The name of a tree form which describes a bonsai with trunk and branches hanging as if cascading from a cliff.

CHEESECLOTH
Meshed cloth that is used to screen out direct sunlight and so on.

CHOKED ROOTS
When roots grow to take up the whole pot, they become suffocated. Repotting prevents this condition.

CLUMP
The name of a tree form in bonsai describing multiple trunks extending from one base.

COMPOUND FERTILIZER
Chemically processed fertilizer.

CUTTING
A method of creating plant stock by cutting a branch or shoot and placing it in soil to put out roots. Plant stock grown in this way are called cuttings.

CUTTING BACK
The task of trimming off stalks, branches and so on from the bud node in order to maintain tree form and restore strength.

DECIDUOUS TREE
A tree which sheds its leaves every winter.

DEHYDRATION/WATER LOSS
The weakened condition of roots and plant stock due to insufficient water.

DORMANT PERIOD
A period such as winter in which plants rest due to temperature, humidity and other conditions being unsuited to their development.

EVERGREEN TREE
Types of trees with foliage that is green all year round.

EXPOSED ROOT
A tree form in which the root protrudes above ground, resembling a solid trunk.

FLOWER BUDS
Buds that form flowers (also known as reproductive shoots). The transformation that occurs to allow flowers to form is called flower differentiation. There are flower buds and leaf buds.

FLOWERING BONSAI
A bonsai classification based on tree type, in this case, bonsai which are grown for their blossoms.

FOREST
A bonsai tree form in which five or more trees are grown together to resemble woodland or forest scenery.

FRUITING BONSAI
A bonsai classification based on tree type, in this case, bonsai which are grown for their fruit.

INFORMAL UPRIGHT
A bonsai tree form whose design is created by its bent, winding trunk.

IMI-EDA (FAULTY/DREADFUL BRANCHES)
Extraneous branches that spoil the attractiveness of a tree, such as backwards branches, tangled branches, branches growing from the same whorl and so on. Trim them off or correct them with wire.

INITIAL RISE/LOWER TRUNK
The section of the trunk between the base and the lowest branch. This is one of the points of note in bonsai.

LARGE BONSAI
A bonsai size category, generally for bonsai over 24 inches (60cm) tall.

LEAF BURN
Damage that occurs to the ends and edges of leaves when direct sunlight causes them to wither.

LEAF CROPPING
The removal of leaves, leaving only the stalk, in order for sunshine to penetrate and new shoots to form.

LEAF CUTTING

Trimming oversized leaves or dense foliage down to a smaller size.

LEAF THINNING

Thinning out overly dense foliage.

LIQUID FERTILIZER

Fertilizer in liquid form, made from compound fertilizer diluted with water. They have an immediate effect.

MAME BACHI (Literally "bean pot")

A pot so small it fits in the palm of a hand.

MEDIUM BONSAI

A bonsai size category, generally for bonsai between 8 and 24 inches (20cm–60cm) tall.

NON-WOODY PERENNIAL BONSAI

Bonsai made from non-woody perennial plants and grasses.

PINALES

A tree species which is also a bonsai classification. Pines, cedars, Chinese junipers and other evergreens can be used to make this category of bonsai.

PINCHING OUT

Using tweezers or fingertips to pinch off new buds before they grow.

PRUNING

Trimming the trunk, branches and leaves of a tree to maintain its health and neaten its form.

REPOTTING

Removing a plant from its pot, tidying the roots, replacing old soil with new and replanting the plant in the pot.

ROOT DECAY

Decay and damage to roots caused by lack of oxygen due to being constantly submerged in water.

SCION

A branch used for cuttings.

SEED BED

Soil in which to sow seeds.

SEEDLING

A plant germinated and raised from seed; plant stock raised from seed.

SMALL BONSAI

A bonsai size category, generally for bonsai under 8 inches (20cm) tall. Bonsai under 4 inches (10cm) in this category are known as mini bonsai and *mame* bonsai.

SMALL TREES

A bonsai classification based on tree type. Bonsai made from deciduous trees, and not Pinales such as Japanese maples, zelkovas and beeches, fall into this category.

SOAKING

A method of watering in which the pot is placed in a container of water in order to take in water from the pot base.

SOLID FERTILIZER

Fertilizer in solid form which is placed on the surface of the soil in a pot, such as fertilizer pellets.

SPHAGNUM MOSS

A type of moss used tp augment soil's ability to hold water and nutrients.

STRAIGHT TRUNK

A bonsai tree form in which a tree with a single trunk extends straight up.

THREE-TRUNK

A bonsai tree form named for its three trunks extending from a single base.

TWIN-TRUNK

A bonsai tree form in which two trunks of different sizes grow from the same base.

WATER BINDING

Compacting of soil and sand due to being watered or soaked in water.

WATER DRAWING

Soaking a cut-off branch to allow it to draw in plenty of water and be used as a cutting.

WINDSWEPT

A bonsai tree form describing a tree leaning in one direction as if its trunk, branches and so on were being blown by the wind.

WIRING/TRAINING WITH WIRE

Winding wire around a trunk or branch in order to create form.

Sprouting walnuts

Published by Tuttle Publishing, an imprint of Periplus Editions (HK) Ltd.

www.tuttlepublishing.com

ISBN 978-4-8053-1438-8

Tsukuru . Sodateru . Kazaru! Chou Mini Bonsai
Copyright © 2014 by Teruki Iwai & Boutique-sha, Inc.
English translation rights arranged with BOUTIQUE-SHA INC.
through Japan UNI Agency, Inc., Tokyo

English Translation © 2017 Periplus Editions (HK) Ltd.
Translated from Japanese by Leeyong Soo

Distributed by

North America, Latin America & Europe
Tuttle Publishing
364 Innovation Drive, North Clarendon,
VT 05759-9436 U.S.A.
Tel: 1 (802) 773-8930; Fax: 1 (802) 773-6993
info@tuttlepublishing.com; www.tuttlepublishing.com

Japan
Tuttle Publishing
Yaekari Building, 3rd Floor, 5-4-12 Osaki,
Shinagawa-ku, Tokyo 141 0032
Tel: (81) 3 5437-0171; Fax: (81) 3 5437-0755
sales@tuttle.co.jp; www.tuttle.co.jp

Asia Pacific
Berkeley Books Pte. Ltd.
61 Tai Seng Avenue #02-12, Singapore 534167
Tel: (65) 6280-1330; Fax: (65) 6280-6290
inquiries@periplus.com.sg; www.periplus.com

Printed in China   1704RR
20 19 18 17   10 9 8 7 6 5 4 3 2 1

TUTTLE PUBLISHING® is a registered trademark of Tuttle Publishing, a division of Periplus Editions (HK) Ltd.

About Tuttle: "Books to Span the East and West"

Our core mission at Tuttle Publishing is to create books which bring people together one page at a time. Tuttle was founded in 1832 in the small New England town of Rutland, Vermont (USA). Our fundamental values remain as strong today as they were then—to publish best-in-class books informing the English-speaking world about the countries and peoples of Asia. The world has become a smaller place today and Asia's economic, cultural and political influence has expanded, yet the need for meaningful dialogue and information about this diverse region has never been greater. Since 1948, Tuttle has been a leader in publishing books on the cultures, arts, cuisines, languages and literatures of Asia. Our authors and photographers have won numerous awards and Tuttle has published thousands of books on subjects ranging from martial arts to paper crafts. We welcome you to explore the wealth of information available on Asia at **www.tuttlepublishing.com**.